xcellence
Education

Building Math Rigor

Problems to Promote Student Thinking

Grade 8
Volume 1

NUMERACY RESOURCE

About the Author

Peggy Neal is a Mathematics Education Specialist for the Capitol Region Education Council (CREC) in Hartford, Connecticut. After 29 years of classroom experience, she joined CREC to provide services centered on creating Common Core math curriculum, modeling conceptual instruction and writing assessments for Common Core curriculum units. She is a frequent presenter for the National Council of Teachers of Mathematics (NCTM), the Association of Teachers of Mathematics in New England (ATMNE) and Connecticut's Association of Teachers of Mathematics in Connecticut (ATOMIC) Annual Conference. At the 2016 ATOMIC Annual Conference, she was awarded the Mari Muri Award in recognition of her lifelong contributions to the teaching of mathematics. The contents of this book are a compilation of the work she has shared with the varied classrooms throughout New England.

Building Math Rigor: Problems to Promote Student Thinking
Grade 8, Volume 1
Copyright ©2017 CREC (Capitol Region Education Council)
All Rights Reserved
www.crec.org

Dear Math Colleague,

Thank you for purchasing CREC's Building Math Rigor Volume 1 developed by math specialist Peggy Neal from CREC's Institute of Teaching and Learning. These math problems can be used in the classroom as a warm-up, a "Do Now" activity, a supplement for a class assignment, a station exercise, part of an assessment, or even as homework!

Here are some **helpful hints** for successful implementation.

Step One: Where do I start with the resource?

1. There are two sections – problems to use for your students, and then problems with the answers. This section contains the answers or, for the Problem Solving and Reasoning sections, at least one possible answer to each problem.

2. Each grade level set of problems is organized by standard. Match the problems from this resource to your instructional unit where the same Common Core Standards are located. This will assure the math content is taught so student success on the problems will occur.

Step Two: What should the teacher do before assigning these problems?

Your instructional unit teaches the common core math content. The problems in Building Math Rigor were designed in a particular format that may not be part of your existing instructional unit. It is important for students that you explicitly teach and model an exemplary solution for problems from each section.

Procedures and Concepts: the true/false or yes/no formatted problems: You may find it helpful to provide a specific area for students to show their work to "prove" the problem is true or false. Scan the QR code below for an example or visit www.crec.org/building-math-rigor/examples

Problem Solving Problems in this section generally are multi-step problems – model an exemplary response. Include a diagram if needed, labels for numbers in the context and a solution sentence that answers the question posed in the problem.

Reasoning Problems in this section fall into two categories: provide the reasoning to justify a claim or find the error in the reasoning provided. Model an exemplary solution for each type of problem. These are best done on chart paper so they become an anchor chart for student reference.

Step Three: When and how should the problems be used in the classroom?

The math problems in this resource should be used several times a week over the entire year. The repeated practice over time will assist students in their success and accuracy with the solution. There are many ways to implement their use!

- **At the beginning of class:**

  During the first 4-5 minutes of math class (sometimes called a warm-up or Do Now) one or two of these problems can engage students and help transition them to think mathematically. This problem from Grade 3 Procedures and Concepts could be a warm-up following instruction on rounding whole numbers:

  Select Yes or No if the following numbers are between 801 and 874.. (3.NBT.1)

Number	Yes	No
810		
851		
799		
870		
899		

  The teacher would ask different students to orally justify their reasoning for choosing Yes or No. Students can show their work and reasoning on white boards.

- **During class:**

  The problems in Building Math Rigor can become a great station activity. Math Stations or Centers provide an opportunity for students to practice and apply skills and strategies taught within the classroom. While students are engaged in meaningful activities, teachers have the opportunity to work individually or with small, flexible groups to meet the individual needs of students.

  This Grade 8 problem could easily be a station activity during a unit on solving equations. Students would practice solving a variety of equations, then sort each equation by its solution.

Sort the following equations into the category that correctly shows the solution of the equation. Write the letter of the equation in the box according to its solution. (8.EE.7)

Equation A	Equation B	Equation C	Equation D	Equation E
$5 = 5(4x - 1)$	$-8x - 7 = -1$	$2(x - 1.25) = -4$	$-6x - 5 = 2x - 9$	$-2 = 4 - 12x$

Solution	Solution
$x = 0.5$	$x = -\dfrac{3}{4}$

- ## As a supplement to a class assignment

  The problems can be used as a supplement to a class assignment. After a lesson in grade 6 focused on finding equivalent ratios, this problem can be part of a guided practice.

  The ratio of chickens to ducks at the farm is 5:3. Select whether each statement is True or False. (6.RP.3)

Statement	True	False
There could be 15 chickens and 12 ducks on the farm.		
There could be 10 chickens and a total of 16 ducks and chickens on the farm.		
There could be 15 ducks and 25 chickens on the farm.		
There could be 50 chickens and 30 ducks on the farm.		
There could be 18 ducks and a total of 48 ducks and chickens on the farm.		

  Either opportunity, station/center activity or a supplement to a lesson, allows students more practice with the particular format found on state/national assessments.

- ## As an assessment item

  If you include some of the problems from Building Math Rigor as part of your instructional unit, then similar problems can be part of a formative assessment, a quiz or as part of a summative assessment. Students need opportunities in class during each instructional unit with the format of the problems presented in Building Math Rigor Volume 1, so the assessment data is focused on the math content.

- ## The problems can also be assigned as homework!

Table of Contents

Grade Level **8**

NUMERACY
RESOURCE

Procedures and Concepts

Expressions and Equations

1. Select True or False for each equation below. (8.EE.4)

Equations	True	False
$1.65 \times 10^{-2} = 0.0165$		
$8.25 \times 10^{5} = 825{,}000$		
$0.423 \times 10^{3} = 423{,}000$		
$2.9 \times 10^{-4} = 0.000029$		

2. Sort the following equations into the category that correctly shows the solution of the equation. (8.EE.7)

Write the **letter** of the equation in the box.

Equation A	Equation B	Equation C	Equation D	Equation E
$5 = 5(4x - 1)$	$-8x - 7 = -1$	$2(x - 1.25) = -4$	$-6x - 5 = 2x - 9$	$-2 = 4 - 12x$

Solution $x = 0.5$	Solution $x = -\dfrac{3}{4}$

3. A framing company makes square frames whose side lengths are integer values.
   Circle **all** the areas that would satisfy this requirement.   (8.EE.2)

64 ft²	32 ft²	0.81 ft²	50 ft²
1 ft²	2.5 ft²	100 ft²	60 ft²

4. Bryan and Bob are both landscapers. Bryan charges $30 for each job plus $15 per hour. Bob charges $5 for each job plus $20 per hour. Use this information to select whether each statement is true or false.   (8.EE.7)

Statement	True	False
For 2 hours of work, Bryan charges more.		
For 6 hours of work, Bob charges less.		
Bob charges $65 for 3 hours of work.		
They charge the same amount of money for 5 hours of work.		
Bryan charges $120 for 8 hours of work.		

5. Select if each equation has No Solution, One Solution or Infinite Solutions.   (8.EE. 7)

Equation	No Solution	One Solution	Infinite Solutions
$6x - 3 - 4x = 2x - 8$			
$-8(4x - 2) = -4(-4 + 8x)$			
$6 - (3x - 4) = -5x + 2$			
$10x + 4 + x = 4 + 5x - 3$			
$4x - (x - 5) = 3x - 5$			

6. Select if $x = -2$ is a solution for each equation or not a solution.   (8.EE. 7)

Equation	$x = -2$ is a solution	$x = -2$ is not a solution
$4x + 10 = 2$		
$11 = 4x + 3$		
$-5x + 6 = 16$		
$x + 8 = 6$		
$-12 = -5x - 2$		

7. After 3 hours of driving Maxwell is 165 miles from home. After 5 hours, Maxwell is 275 miles from home. Maxwell makes a graph of the data.   (8.EE.5)
Select whether each statement is True or False.

Statement	True	False
The slope of the line is $\frac{45}{1}$.		
After 1.5 hours, Maxwell was 82.5 miles from home.		
The relationship between time driving and distance travelled is proportional.		
Maxwell travels at a constant speed of 55 mph.		
The y-intercept for this relationship is (0, 55)		

8. The Holden Corporation sells items that are shaped like cubes. Select Yes or No if the volumes below represent cubes with integer side lengths.   (8.EE.2)

Volumes	Yes	No
27 in.³		
6.25 m³		
1000 cm.³		
33 in.³		
4.8 yd³		
8 in.³		

9. A shipping company has a stack of boxes. The stack measures x boxes wide, x boxes high and x boxes long. Select Yes or No if the equations could represent the total number of boxes. (8.EE.2)

Equations	Yes	No
$64 = x^3$		
$8000 = x^3$		
$24 = x^3$		
$100 = x^3$		
$125 = x^3$		
$9 = x^3$		

10. Select True or False for each inequality below. (8.EE.4)

Equations	True	False
$4.7 \times 10^4 > 4.7 \times 10^{-4}$		
$3.2 \times 10^{-2} < 3.2 \times 10^{-3}$		
$1.4 \times 10^{-1} > 1.4 \times 10^{-2}$		
$2.5 \times 10^{-5} < 2.5 \times 10^{-1}$		

11. Select True or False for each equation below. (8.EE.1)

Equations	True	False
$2^{-3} \times 2^{-2} = 2^{-5} = \dfrac{1}{32}$		
$3^{-7} \times 3^4 = 3^{-2} = \dfrac{1}{9}$		
$5^2 \times 5^{-4} = 5^{-2} = \dfrac{1}{25}$		
$4^{-1} \times 4^{-2} = 4^{-3} = \dfrac{1}{12}$		

12. Sort the following equations into the category that correctly shows the solution of the equation. (8.EE.7)

Write the **letter** of the equation in the box.

Equation A	Equation B	Equation C	Equation D	Equation E
$5x + 2.5 = 10$	$2(x - 2) = -2x - 10$	$-3 = -8x + 9$	$-x + 4.5 = -4x$	$6x + 4 = 4x + 7$

Solution $x = -1.5$	Solution $x = \dfrac{3}{2}$

13. Sort each expression into the correct category. (8.EE.1)

Write the letter of the expression in the box.

Expression A	Expression B	Expression C
$\dfrac{4^9}{4^{10}}$	$\dfrac{4^{10}}{4^9}$	$4^6(4^{-4})$

Expression D	Expression E	Expression F
$(4^2 \cdot 4)^0$	$(-4)^3$	$\dfrac{4^{-2}}{4^{-4}}$

Less than 4	Equal to 4	Greater than 4

14. Circle all the equations that are parallel to the line: $y = 1.5x + 2$.   (8.EE.6)

$$4 = -1.5x - y \qquad y = \frac{6}{4}x + 2.1 \qquad y = \frac{3}{2}x \qquad y - 1.5x = 5$$

15. Otto buys two picture frames. Each picture frame is shaped like an equilateral polygon as shown in the picture below. The two picture frames have the same perimeter. Select whether each statement is True or False.   (8.EE.7)

Statement	True	False
The value of x is 12.		
The side length of the rhombus is 9.		
The equation $3(x + 5) - 4(x+2) = 0$ can be used to solve for x.		
The perimeter of the triangular picture frame is 36.		

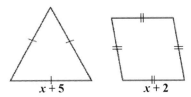

$x + 5$ $x + 2$

16. Ramone and Felix are both electricians. Ramone charges a flat fee of $63 plus $36 per hour. Felix charges $50 per hour. Select whether each statement below is True or False.   (8.EE.7)

Statement	True	False
For 3 hours of work Ramone charges $108.		
For 7 hours of work, Felix charges $350.		
Both electricians charge the same amount for 4 hours of work.		
The equation $50x = 63 + 36x$ can be used to find the number of hours, x, for which the total cost is the same for both electricians.		
Ramone's total cost is less than Felix's total cost for a job that takes 3 hours to complete.		

17. The perimeter of a rectangular garden is 56 feet. The length of the garden is $(3x + 1)$ feet and the width of the garden is $(2x - 3)$ feet.　　　　(8.EE.7)
Select if each statement below is True or False.

Statement	True	False
The width of the garden is 9 feet.		
The equation $(3x + 1) + (2x - 3) = 56$ can be solved to find the value of x.		
The length of the garden is 19 feet.		
The equation $56 - 2(3x + 1) = 2(2x - 3)$ can be solved to find the value of x.		
The garden is a square.		

18. Select if each equation has No Solution, One Solution or Infinite Solutions.　　　　(8.EE. 7)

Equation	No Solution	One Solution	Infinite Solutions
$7 - 2x - 3 = 2(2 - x)$			
$4x - (-2x + 4) = 10x + 4$			
$-6x - 3x + x - 2 = 2(-4x - 1)$			
$5 - 4(2x - 3) = -8x + 7$			
$-5(2x - 3) = 4x - 9$			

19. Sort the following pairs of equations into the category that correctly describes if the lines are parallel or perpendicular.

(8.EE.8)

Write the **letter** of the equations in the box.

Equations A	Equations B	Equations C	Equations D	Equations E
$y = 2x - 3$ $y = -\dfrac{1}{2}x + 2$	$y = -0.5x + 8$ $y - 4 = 2x$	$y = -3x - 2$ $y = -3x + 5$	$y = 2.5x - 1$ $y = -0.4x$	$y = \dfrac{8}{2}x + 12$ $y = 4x - 4$

Parallel Lines	Perpendicular Lines

20. Select Yes or No if the point (2,3) is a solution for each system of equations in the table below.

(8.EE. 8)

Equations	Yes (2,3) is a Solution	No (2,3) is not a Solution
$y = x + 1$ $y = 0.5x + 2$		
$y - x = 1$ $2x - 1 = y$		
$y + x = 5$ $2y - 2x = 1$		
$y = 3x - 3$ $y = 5x - 7$		
$y = 2x - 1$ $y = 3x$		

21. Select Equal or Not Equal if each equations in the table below is equal to the equation:
$$k = 3m - 6.$$

(8.EE. 7)

Equations	Equal to $k = 3m - 6$	Not Equal to $k = 3m - 6$
$\frac{1}{3}k + 2 = m$		
$\frac{k+6}{3} = m$		
$m = \frac{6-k}{3}$		
$k + 6 = m$		
$\frac{k}{3} + 2 = m$		

22. Circle all the slopes that are equal to the slope between the two points:

(8.EE.6)

(2, -2) and (8, 1)

$$\frac{4}{2} \qquad \frac{3}{6} \qquad \frac{1}{2} \qquad 0.5 \qquad \frac{-5}{-10} \qquad 2$$

23. Select Yes or No if each point lies on the graph of: $6x - 4 = y$.

(8.EE.6)

Point	Yes on the graph	Not on the graph
(2, 10)		
(1, 2)		
(0, -4)		
(-5, -26)		
(-2, -16)		

24. Select Yes or No if each equation in the table can be used to represent this problem:
In 10 years, Rasha will be 49 years old. Let a = Rasha's age now.

(8.EE.7)

Equation	Yes	Not
$49 + a = 10$		
$10 + a = 49$		
$a = 49 - 10$		
$10 - a = 49$		
$49 - a = 10$		

25. A system of equations has No Solution. Select if each statement below is True or False.

(8.EE.8)

Statement	True	False
Both equations have the same slopes but different y-intercepts.		
The lines are parallel.		
Both equations have the different slopes and different y-intercepts.		
The lines intersect at one point.		
Both lines pass through the origin.		

26. Select Yes or No if each point is a solution to: $\frac{x}{4} - 3 = y$.

(8.EE.6)

Point	Yes is a solution	No is not a solution
(4, -2)		
(-8, -5)		
(1, 1)		
(20, 2)		
(12, 0)		

27. Select True or False for each statement below.

(8.EE.6)

Statement	True	False
The slope of a line with the points (1, 2) and (4, 3) on it is positive.		
The y-intercept in $y=3x-1$ is the point (0, 1)		
The unit rate of $y = \frac{2}{3}x$ is $\frac{2}{3}$.		
The line y= -3 has a negative slope.		
The equation $x - y = 5$ has a positive slope.		
The y-intercept of $x - y = 5$ is the point (0, -5)		

28. Sort the following cards into the correct category. Write the letter of the card in the category.

(8.EE.6)

Card A	Card B	Card C	Card D	Card E	Card F
$y = \dfrac{7}{4}x - 2$	$y = -\dfrac{5}{6}x$	$\dfrac{-7}{8}x = y$	$y = -7$	$y = 3x + 4$	$4 = y - x$

Positive Slope	Negative Slope	Zero Slope

29. Select Yes or No if each problem below has a slope equal to the slope in the equation:

$$y = \frac{3}{6}x + 4$$

(8.EE.6)

Yes	No	Problem
		$y = \dfrac{-1}{2}x - 5$
		Points (7, 2) and (-1, -2)
		$y = 0.5x + 2.$
		$\dfrac{-5}{10}x + y = 6$
		$y = 3 - 2x$

30. Select True or False for each statement.

(8.EE.6)

Statement	True	False
The slope of $y = \frac{3}{4}x + 2$ is steeper than of $y = -\frac{3}{4}x + 2$.		
The y-intercepts are the same in the equations: $y = \frac{4}{5}x + 3$ and $y = 0.8x - 3$.		
A line with a slope of zero is a horizontal line.		
$x + y = 8$ is the same equation as $y = 8 - x$.		
The slope of $y = -\frac{7}{8}x + 1$ is steeper than the slope of $y = -\frac{2}{3}x + 2$.		

Functions

1. The cost at Playland to use the Internet includes a flat fee plus a constant rate per minute, as shown in the table below.   (8.F.4)

Time (minutes), x	1	5	10	15
Total Cost ($), y	$1.70	$2.50	$3.50	$4.50

Select if each statement is True or False.

Statement	True	False
8 minutes of Internet use costs $3.00.		
The constant rate of change is $0.20 per minute.		
The flat fee is $1.50.		
Each minute of Internet use costs $1.50.		

2. The table shows the cost of buying different amounts of ham at the deli. The total cost is a direct variation of the number of pounds purchased.   (8.F.4)

Weight (lbs.), x	2	4	10
Cost, $, y	13	26	65

What is the constant of proportionality? _____

Write an equation in $y = mx$ form to represent this situation. _____

3. Use the graph to determine if each statement below is True or False.   (8.F.4)

Statement	True	False
The slope of the line is $\frac{75}{2}$.		
In 4 hours, the Townsend family travelled 150 miles.		
It took the Townsend family about 1.5 hours to travel 27 miles.		
The y-intercept is (0, 0).		

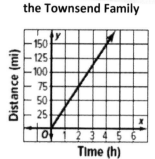

Distance Traveled by the Townsend Family

4. An appliance store is having a 20% sale on all items in the store. Mr. Grande has a coupon for $15 off. The function $f(x) = 0.8x - 15$ represents the final cost after the discount and coupon are applied for an item priced x dollars. Complete the function table below.   (8.F.1, 8.F.4)

Input	Output
$150	
	$65
$372	
	$437

5. Circle each table below if it is a function.

        (8.F.1)

Table One

x	y
-8	0
-3	5
2	10
4	10

Table Two

x	y
-2	4
-2	3
0	2
2	1

Table Three

x	y
-1	4
0	8
1	12
2	16

Table Four

x	y
0	2
1	4
2	6
2	7

Table Five

x	y
-2	2
-1	1
0	0
1	1

6. Select Yes or No if the following points are correct values for the function: $y = \frac{1}{4}x$.

(8.F.1)

Points	Yes	No
(4, 1)		
(-4, -4)		
(0, 0)		
(3, 12)		
(-2, -0.5)		

7. Select if the slope of the equation given is greater or not greater than the slope of the line in the graph.

(8.F.1)

Equation	Slope is Greater	Slope is Not Greater
$y = x + 6$		
$y = -3x$		
$y = 0.8x + 3$		
$y = \frac{1}{2}x - 2$		
$y = 2.6x + 1$		

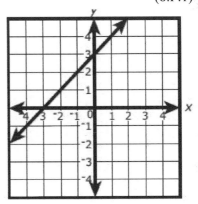

Geometry

1. $\overline{CD}$ and $\overline{AB}$ are plotted on the coordinate plane below. Select whether each statement is True or False.   (8.G.1)

Statement	True	False
The image of point C reflected over the y-axis is (-1, -2).		
The slope of $\overline{AB}$ = the slope of $\overline{CD}$ but the direction is different.		
$\overline{AB} \perp \overline{CD}$		
$\overline{CD}$ can be mapped onto $\overline{AB}$ by a reflection over the y-axis then a reflection over the x-axis.		
The slope of $\overline{AB}$ is positive and the slope of $\overline{CD}$ is negative.		

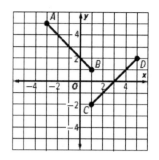

2. A triangular flag GHF is mapped on the coordinate plane below. The flag is reflected across the y-axis and is then translated 4 units down and 3 units right to form   .   (8.G.2)
        Select whether each statement is True or False.

Statement	True	False
The image of point G is G' (-4,1).		
The image of point H is H' (2, -3).		
The image of point F is F' (0,-1).		
The slopes of $\overline{FH}$ and $\overline{F'H'}$ are reciprocals.		
Triangle GHF is congruent to triangle G'H'F'		

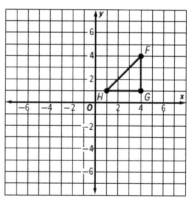

3. Beef stew is available in two different-sized cans. Nick's Beef Stew is a 90-ounce can and is sold for $12.50 per can. The can has a diameter of 6 inches and a height of 4.2 inches. Ray's Beef Stew is a 55-ounce can and is sold for $6.02 per can. This can has a diameter of 4.2 inches and a height of 6 inches. Select whether each statement is True or False.   (8.G.9)

Statement	True	False
The volume of Nick's Beef Stew is about 118.69 cubic inches.		
Ray's Beef Stew is the better buy because it is about 11 cents per ounce.		
The volume of Ray's Beef Stew is about 3 times the volume of Nick's Beef Stew.		
The difference in the price per ounce of the two cans is about 3 cents.		

4. A square is mapped on a coordinate plane. Mary uses square *SPRQ* and the rule (-0.5*x*, -0.5*y*) to draw another square.   (8.G.3)

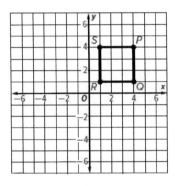

Select whether each statement is True or False.

Statement	True	False
The square *S'P'R'Q'* is smaller in size than square *SPRQ*.		
The image of point P is *P'* (-2, -2).		
The image of point R is *R'* (0.5, 0.5)		
Square *SPRQ* and its image are congruent polygons.		
The length of *SP* is twice the length of *S'P'*.		

5. Triangle ABC and Triangle DEF are plotted on a coordinate plane. (8.G.1)

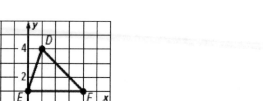

Select whether each statement is True or False.

Statement	True	False
The area of Triangle *DEF* is 12 square units.		
The height of triangle *ABC* is 3.		
Triangle *ABC* can be mapped onto Triangle *DEF* by the translation $(x + 3, y + 5)$		
The length of *BC* = the length of *EF*.		
Triangle *DEF* can be mapped onto Triangle *ABC* by the translation $(x - 5, y - 3)$		

6. Use the description of each triangle to determine if it is a right triangle or not.

(8.G.7)

Statement	Yes forms a right triangle	No does not form a right triangle
Triangle with side lengths 6, 6 and $6\sqrt{2}$.		
Perimeter of 12, two sides are 4 and 5.		
Triangle with sides 5, 8 and 13.		
Perimeter of 36, two sides are 9 and 12.		
Triangle with sides 10, 5 and $5\sqrt{5}$		

The Number System

1. Select whether the number described in each statement is rational or irrational.

(8.NS.1)

Statement	Rational	Irrational
Jack calculates each side length of a square as $3\sqrt{16}$ meters.		
The length of a rope measures $42.\overline{6}$ cm.		
The circumference of a circular frame is 5π inches.		
The depth of a canyon is -85.75 feet.		

2. Mrs. Foster gave her math students a task work 100 points. (8.NS.1)

These are 4 of the student scores:

- ☐ Sylvester earned a score of 88.6%,
- ☐ Dana earned a score of $\frac{89}{100}$ points,
- ☐ Irma earned a score of $\sqrt{7569}$ points
- ☐ Paul earned a score of that was 1.4 percent less than Sylvester's percent.

Plot these points on the number line below. Use the first letter of the student's name to label the points.

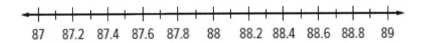

3. The number line below shows four points labeled *A*, *B*, *C* and *D*. Select whether each statement is True or False. (8.NS.2)

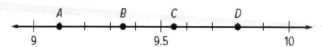

Statement	True	False
The value of $\sqrt{86.49}$ is between points *A* and *B*.		
The coordinate of point C is greater than $\sqrt{95}$.		
The coordinate of Point D is less than $\sqrt{99}$.		

4. Select whether each statement is True or False. (8.NS.2)

Statement	True	False
$\sqrt{5+16}$ is irrational.		
0.5274 is rational.		
$0.\overline{36}$ is irrational.		
0.234234234…is irrational.		
$\sqrt{2}$ is irrational.		

5. The number line shows four points labeled *A*, *B*, *C* and *D*. Select whether each statement is True or False. (8.NS.2)

Statement	True	False
The value of $\sqrt{63}$ is between points *C* and *D*.		
The coordinate of point B is greater than $\sqrt{50}$.		
The coordinate of Point A is less than $\sqrt{55}$.		

Grade Level **8**

NUMERACY
RESOURCE

Problem Solving

The Number System

1. Tanya and Vinny are having a contest to see who can rake the greater area of lawn over one week. The table shows the area in acres they raked each day. (8.NS.1)

Day	Tanya	Vinny
Sunday	$1\frac{1}{4}$ acres	$\frac{6}{5}$ acres
Monday	0.6 acres	$\frac{1}{2}$ acre
Tuesday	30% of an acre	0.34 of an acre
Wednesday	20% of an acre	$\frac{1}{3}$ acre
Thursday	$\frac{13}{25}$ of an acre	0.58 acres
Friday	75% of an acre	$\frac{2}{3}$ of an acre
Saturday	1 acre	1.1 acres

Part A: Sort each day into one of the two categories according to who raked more that day. Write the day of the week in the correct category.

Tanya raked more acres	Vinny raked more acres

Part B: Who won the contest? _____
Part C: How much more did the winner rake? _____

2. Graph the numbers at their approximate locations on the number line. (8.NS.2)
   Label the location using the point letter.

Point A = $\sqrt{66}$ Point B= $-\sqrt{15}$ Point C= $\sqrt{35}$ Point D= $-\sqrt{10}$

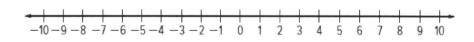

Expressions and Equations

1. Kevin's Cab Company charges $6.00 per ride plus $2.50 per mile traveled. Kathy's Cab Company charges $3.00 per ride and $3.00 per mile traveled. (8.EE.7)

Part A: Write an equation to find *m*, the number of miles for which the total cost is the same for both companies.

Part B: Solve your equation to find the number of miles.

2. David purchased a storage cube that has a volume of 12 cubic feet. He wants to put the cube on a shelf that is 25 inches below the ceiling. (8.EE.2)

Will the cube fit? _____
Explain your reasoning.

3. Polly ran 3 times as many miles as Michael. Michael ran 10 fewer miles than Polly. The number of miles run by each person can be modeled by the system of equations shown below, where *y* represents Polly's miles and *x* represents the number of miles Michael ran. (8.EE.8)

$$y = 3x \qquad y = x + 10$$

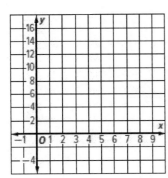

Part A: Graph the equations on the coordinate plane. Label the intersection.

Part B: What is the solution to the system? _____

4. Tracy and her younger sister, Heather, are running a 120-meter race. Tracy runs at a steady rate of 3.5 meters per second. Heather runs at a steady rate of 2 meters per second.

(8.EE.5, 8.EE.7)

Part A: How long will it take each person to finish the race?

Part B: Tracy wants to win the race but only by 5 seconds. She is going to give her sister a 30 meter, 40 meter or 50 meter head start.

Which head start allows Tracy to win the race within 5 seconds of her sister's time?

5. The area of each small square in the figures below is 49 square units. (8.EE.2)

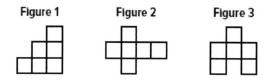

Figure 1   Figure 2   Figure 3

Part A: What do you notice about the areas of the 3 figures? _____

_____

Part B: What is the perimeter of each figure? Show your work here:

6. Franklin works as a sales person. He earns $600 per week plus an 8% commission on his total sales.   (8.EE.7)

Part A: Last week he had a total sales of $4,000. What was his total earnings?

Part B: This week he wants his sales to increase from last week to this week by an additional $800. How much more will his total earnings be this week compared to last week?

7. Julia has a storage cube with a volume of 27 cubic feet. She has a shelf that is 35 inches from the ceiling.   (8.EE.2)

       Will the cube fit? _____

       Explain how you know.

8. What is the measure of the largest angle in this triangle?

                                     (8.EE.7)

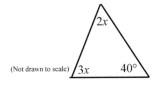

                          Show your work here.

(Not drawn to scale)

9. The chess team has 35 female members. The ratio of females to males on the team is 7 to 5. How many members are on the chess team in all? (8.EE.7)

Show your work here.

10. A park in Canada is in the shape of a rectangle. The length is 2.4×10^5 feet and the width is 3.1×10^3 feet. One acre measures 4.356×10^4 square feet. (8.EE.4)

About how many acres does the park cover? Round your answer to the nearest hundredth.

Show your work here.

11. At one sports club, $\frac{5}{6}$ of the people were playing volleyball. After 2 more people joined the people playing volleyball, there was a total of 27 people playing volleyball. How many people in all were at the sports club? (8.EE.7)

Part A: Circle all the equations that can be used to solve this problem.

$\frac{5}{6}x - 2 = 27$ $\qquad$ $\frac{5}{6}x = 25$ $\qquad$ $\frac{5}{6}(x + 2) = 27$

$27 - 2 = \frac{5}{6}x$ $\qquad$ $\frac{5}{6}x + 2x = 27$ $\qquad$ $27 = \frac{5}{6}x + 2$

Part B: How many people in all were at the sports club?

12. The table shows expressions to represent the number of middle school students enrolled in different clubs. The number of students enrolled in the Drama and Tech Clubs equals the students in the Adventure and Math Clubs.   (8.EE.7)

Club	Number of Students
Drama Club	2n - 14
Tech Club	2(3n -15)
Adventure Club	$\frac{2}{3}n + 2$
Math Club	5n - 4

How many students are in each Club? How many student in all are in the 4 Clubs?

Show your work here.

13. The table below shows the total distance Mrs. Brockton drove last week.   (8.EE.7)

Day	Sunday	Monday	Tuesday	Wednesday	Thursday	Friday	Saturday
Miles	10.5	9.75	9.5	10.25	10.75	12	9.25

The total distance Mrs. Brockton drove last week is $\frac{3}{4}$ of the total distance she drove this week.

Part A: Write an equation that can be used to find the total distance, *d*, Mrs. Brockton drove this week.

Part B: Solve your equation to find the total miles driven this week.

14. Marty's Online Shopping Company uses boxes like the one shown below to ship purchases to their customers. (8.EE.7)

Part A: The shipping box needs 3,528 square centimeters of cardboard to make its six sides, without overlap. What is the height of the box?
Use the formula for the surface area of a prism $SA = 2wh + 2lw + 2lh$ to write an equation, then find the box height.

36 cm

24 cm

Part B: Would packing material with a volume of 13,000 cubic centimeters fit inside this box? Explain why or why not.

15. At Hastings School, $\frac{1}{6}$ of the girls had retakes of their school photo. Twenty girls had retakes done. Eight boys had retakes, which was $\frac{2}{15}$ of the boys at the school. How many students are at Hastings School?

(8.EE.7)

Show your work here.

16. The height of a tree after x years is $1.8x + 3$. How many years will it take for the tree to be 30 feet tall?   (8.EE.7)

Show your work here.

17. A boat traveled x miles per hour upstream for 4 hours. On the return trip, it traveled 2.5 mph faster. The return trip took 3 hours. What was the round trip distance the boat traveled?

(8.EE.7)

Show your work here.

18. Shari wrote the number of hours she ran each day this week in the chart.

(8.EE.7)

Day	Miles
Monday	1.5
Tuesday	0.75
Wednesday	1.25
Thursday	2.5
Friday	x

How many miles does she need to run to average 1.6 miles over the five days?

Show your work here.

19. The table shows Jolene's first six quiz scores in science. After Quiz 1 she stayed each week for extra help with the teacher. What is the rate of change from week 2 to week 6?

(8.EE.7)

Weekly Quiz Number	Score out of 100 points
1	70
2	68
3	72
4	75
5	81
6	93

Functions

1. Joan kicked a ball. The path of the ball can be modeled by the equation:
   $$y = 1.5x^2.$$ (8.F.3)

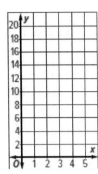

   Part A: Make a table of values of x from 0 to 3.

   Part B: Graph the path of the kicked ball.

   Part C: Is the graph linear? _____

   Justify your answer with at least 2 reasons.

2. The height of a dime dropped from a 144-foot tall building roof is modeled by the function $h = -16t^2 + 144$, where t is the time in seconds and h is the height of the dime as it falls to the ground. (8.F.1, 8.F.3)

   Part A: Complete the table of values for the dime as it falls.

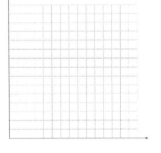

Time, t	0	0.5	1	1.5	2	2.5	3
Height, h							

   Part B: Graph the function on the coordinate plane to the right.

   Part C: How long does it take for the dime to reach the ground?

3. Mr. Stevens is filling his child's pool. The pool has a capacity of 240 gallons. Every minute, a constant 4.5 gallons of water flows into the pool.

(8.F.4)

Part A: Complete the table to show the number of gallons or minutes.

Minutes	Gallons
1	
2	
5	
	36
	45

Part B: How many gallons of water will be added after 12 minutes? _____

Part C: The pool started with 126 gallons of water. After 12 minutes of filling the pool, what percent of the full capacity does the water in the pool represent?

4. Kate and Ruth ran a race. Ruth gets a 44 foot head start. The distance, y (in feet) Ruth runs after x seconds is represented by the linear function: $y = 16x + 44$. The table shows the distances Kate runs.

(8.F.2)

Time, sec. x	2	4	10
Distance, feet y	36	72	190

Part A: Who runs faster?

Explain how you know.

Part B: After how many seconds will they be at the same distance?

Show your work here.

Part C: At what distance will they be in the same place?

Show your work here.

Geometry and Statistics

1. The picture below shows how a pole broke during a winter storm.   (8.G.7)

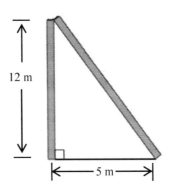

How tall was the original pole?

Show your work.

12 m

5 m

2. Donna dilates the rectangle below using a scale factor of 25%.

(8.G.4)

12 cm

20 cm

What is the area of the dilated rectangle?

3. A rectangular sports arena measures 100 yards by 50 yards. Debbie ran from one corner to the opposite corner along the diagonal of the rectangle. Arthur ran along the length and then the width to the opposite corner.   (8.G.7)

Part A: Who ran further?

Part B: By how many more yards?
Round your answer to the nearest tenth of a yard.

4. Benita surveys some friends to see the number of hours they studied for the History test. The results are recorded in the table. (8.SP.1)

Time (h)	4	0	2.5	1	3	1.5
Test Score	95	65	75	85	90	80

Part A: Construct a scatterplot of the data.

Part B: Describe one pattern you see in the data.

_____

_____

_____

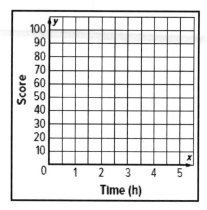

5. Maple Avenue and Pine Street are parallel. Ridge Road is a straight road that crosses each of them. The town planner needs to find the measures of the angles at each intersection.

(8.G.5)

Find the measures of the labeled angles.

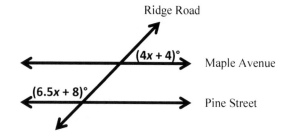

6. An apartment building measures 36 feet by 29 feet as shown in the picture below.

(8.G.7)

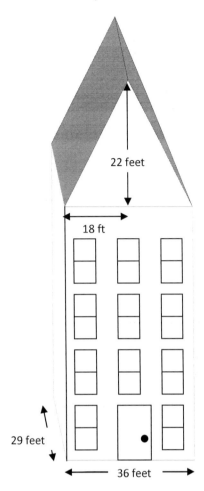

The owner needs to cover the roof, the shaded section in the picture, with shingles. A package of shingles costs $50 and will cover a 15-foot by 15-foot area.

How much will it cost for enough packages of shingles to cover the roof? _____

Show your work here.

7. A triangle has two sides whose measures are 15 feet and 25 feet. The perimeter of the triangle is 60 feet.

(8.G.7)

Is the triangle a right triangle?

Show your work here.

8. The area of the square pictured below is 1,296 in².

(8.G.7)

$4x$

What is the length of the side of the square?

9. Two planes are flying in the same direction towards the same tower at the same airport. Plane A's altitude is 6.4 km. high. Plane B is 2 km further away from the airport tower and its altitude is 2.8 km.

(8.G.7)

Which plane is further in distance from the base of the airport tower?

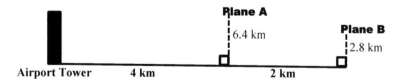

Grade Level 8

NUMERACY
RESOURCE

Reasoning

1. Rodney had to compare the following numbers. (8.EE.1)

$$\text{Number A} = 5 \times 10^{-2} \qquad \text{Number B} = 3 \times 10^{-4}$$

Rodney says Number B is greater because the negative exponents just mean the numbers have a negative value. The exponent 10^4 is larger in Number B than the exponent 10^2 in Number A so

$$5 \times 10^{-2} < 3 \times 10^{-4}.$$

Explain what math mistake Rodney made and write the correct comparison.

2. Molly had to find $\sqrt{1681}$. Her work is shown below.

Step 1 $\qquad \sqrt{1681} = \sqrt{1600} + \sqrt{81}$

Step 2 $\qquad\qquad = 40 + 9$

Step 3 $\qquad \sqrt{1681} = 49$

Explain the math mistake Molly made. Provide the correct solution.

3. A square table has an area of 39 square feet. Joey says the side length has to be between 7.5 and 8 feet. Explain if Joey's thinking is correct or not. (8.NS.2)

4. Justin says that you can use the Commutative property for multiplication with square roots. His example is shown below: (8.NS.2)

$3\sqrt{2}$ has the same value as $2\sqrt{3}$.

Explain if Justin's thinking is correct or not.

5. George had to simplify the following problem. His work is shown below. (8.EE.1)

$$\frac{3^{-2}}{3^{-4}} =$$

Step one: $\frac{1}{3^2} \times \frac{3^4}{1}$

Step two: $\frac{1}{6} \times \frac{12}{1}$

Step three: $\frac{12}{6}$

Step four: 2

Part A: Which step did George make his <u>first</u> mistake? _____

Part B: What math mistake did George make? _____

_____

Part C: Provide the correct solution and work.

6. Mario's solution to the equation $3y + 8 = 7y + 11$ is shown below.

(8.EE.7)

$$3y + 8 = 7y + 11$$

Step one: $\quad -3y \qquad -3y$

Step two: $\qquad 8 = 4y + 11$

$\qquad\qquad -8 \qquad\quad -8$

Step three: $\qquad 4y = 3$

Step four: $\qquad \dfrac{4y}{4} = \dfrac{3}{4}$

Step five: $\qquad y = \dfrac{3}{4}$

Part A: What step did Mario make his <u>first</u> math mistake? _____

Part B: What math mistake did he make? _____

_____

Part C: Provide the correct solution.

7. Nancy's solution to an equation is shown below.

(8.EE.7)

$$6(x - 3) = 4x - 7$$

Step one: $\quad 6x - 3 = 4x - 7$

Step two: $\quad -4x \qquad -4x$

Step three: $\quad 2x - 3 = 7$

$\qquad\qquad\quad +3 \ +3$

Step four: $\quad 2x \quad = 10$

Step five: $\qquad \dfrac{2x}{2} = \dfrac{10}{2}$

Step six: $\qquad x = 5$

Part A: What step did Nancy make her <u>first</u> math mistake? _____

Part B: What math mistake did she make? _____

_____

Part C: Provide the correct solution.

8. Mr. Kroner has a 25-foot ladder and a 30-foot ladder. He claims if you position the 30-foot ladder 15 feet away from the bottom of a building, it will reach no higher than the 25-foot ladder positioned 10 feet away from the bottom of the building.   (8.G.7)

Is Mr. Kroner correct?

Explain how you know.

9. Candace's solution to an equation is shown below.

(8.EE.7)

$$-0.5(20x - 6) - 4 = 17$$

Step one: $-9x - 6 - 4 = 17$
Step two: $-9x - 10 = 17$

Step three: $-9x - 10 = 17$
                $+10 \quad +10$
Step four: $-9x \quad = 27$

Step five: $\dfrac{-9x}{-9} = \dfrac{27}{-9}$

Step six: $x = -3$

Part A: What step did Candace make her <u>first</u> math mistake? _____

Part B: What math mistake did she make? _____

Part C: Provide the correct solution.

10. Alex is making a flag in the shape of a trapezoid. The fabric to make the flag has

an area of 56.25 square inches. The formula for finding the area of a trapezoid is: (8.EE.7)

$$A = \frac{1}{2} h(b_1 + b_2).$$

Alex says if he doubles the longer base, then the area of the flag will also double.

Explain if his thinking is correct.

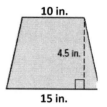
10 in.

4.5 in.

15 in.

11. Lucy is finding the volume of a cube with an edge length of 4ab. Her work is shown below.
     (8.EE.1)

Step one: $V = (4ab)^3$

Step two: $V = (4^3)(a^3)(b^3)$

Step three: $V = 12\ a^3b^3$

Part A: Explain what math mistake Lucy made. _____

Part B: Provide the correct solution.

12. The planet Venus is about 1.1×10^8 km from the sun. The planet Mercury is about 5.8×10^7 km from the sun.

(8.EE.4)

Rona says Mercury is about 5 times farther from the sun than Venus because $5.8 \div 1.1$ is about 5.

     Part A: Explain what math mistake Rona made. _____

     Part B: Provide the correct solution.

13. Harlan says that a triangle with sides that measure 8 cm and 6 cm whose perimeter is 24 cannot be a right triangle because $6^2 + 8^2$ does not equal 24^2.

(8.G.7)

     Part A: Explain what math mistake Harlan made. _____

     Part B: Provide the correct solution.

14. Devon says that 5 + (*xy*) is equal to (5+ *x*) (5+*y*) because it is an example of the Distributive Property.

(8.EE.7)

Part A: Explain what math mistake Devon made. _____

Part B: Provide the correct solution.

15. Vivian and Betsy are writing equations for the line that passes through the points

(-6, 0) and (0. -2).   Their work is shown below.

(8.EE.7)

Vivian's Work	Betsy's Work
$m = \dfrac{2}{6}$ and $b = 2$	$m = \dfrac{-2}{6}$ and the *y*-intercept is 0
so the equation is	so the equation is:
$y = \dfrac{2}{6}x + 2$	$y = \dfrac{-2}{6}x$

Part A: Explain what math error each person made.

Vivian's math error: _____

Betsy's math error: _____

Part B: Provide the correct solution.

Grade Level **8**

NUMERACY
RESOURCE

Procedures and Concepts
ANSWERS

Expressions and Equations

1. Select True or False for each equation below. (8.EE.4)

Equations	True	False
$1.65 \times 10^{-2} = 0.0165$		
$8.25 \times 10^{5} = 825{,}000$		
$0.423 \times 10^3 = 423{,}000$		
$2.9 \times 10^{-4} = 0.000029$		

Answers:
True
True
False
False

2. Sort the following equations into the category that correctly shows the solution of the equation. (8.EE.7)

Write the **letter** of the equation in the box.

Equation A	Equation B	Equation C	Equation D	Equation E
$5 = 5(4x - 1)$	$-8x - 7 = -1$	$2(x - 1.25) = -4$	$-6x - 5 = 2x - 9$	$-2 = 4 - 12x$

Solution $x = 0.5$	Solution $x = -\dfrac{3}{4}$

Answers
Solution $x = 0.5$
   Cards A, D and E
Solution $x = -\dfrac{3}{4}$
Cards B and C

3. A framing company makes square frames whose side lengths are integer values.
   Circle **all** the areas that would satisfy this requirement. (8.EE.2)

64 ft²	32 ft²	0.81 ft²	50 ft²
1 ft²	2.5 ft²	100 ft²	60 ft²

Answers
Circle: 64 ft² 1 ft² 100 ft²

4. Bryan and Bob are both landscapers. Bryan charges $30 for each job plus $15 per hour. Bob charges $5 for each job plus $20 per hour. Use this information to select whether each statement is true or false. (8.EE.7)

Statement	True	False
For 2 hours of work, Bryan charges more.		
For 6 hours of work, Bob charges less.		
Bob charges $65 for 3 hours of work.		
They charge the same amount of money for 5 hours of work.		
Bryan charges $120 for 8 hours of work.		

Answers:
 True
 False
 True
 True
 False

5. Select if each equation has No Solution, One Solution or Infinite Solutions. (8.EE. 7)

Equation	No Solution	One Solution	Infinite Solutions
$6x - 3 - 4x = 2x - 8$			
$-8(4x - 2) = -4(-4 + 8x)$			
$6 - (3x - 4) = -5x + 2$			
$10x + 4 + x = 4 + 5x - 3$			
$4x - (x - 5) = 3x - 5$			

Answers:
No Solution
Infinite Solutions
One Solution
One Solution
No Solution

6. Select if $x = -2$ is a solution for each equation or not a solution.　　(8.EE. 7)

Equation	$x= -2$ is a solution	$x= -2$ is not a solution
$4x + 10 = 2$		
$11 = 4x + 3$		
$-5x + 6 = 16$		
$x + 8 = 6$		
$-12 = -5x -2$		

Answers:
Yes
No
Yes
Yes
No

7. After 3 hours of driving Maxwell is 165 miles from home. After 5 hours, Maxwell is 275 miles from home. Maxwell makes a graph of the data.　　(8.EE.5)
Select whether each statement is True or False.

Statement	True	False
The slope of the line is $\frac{45}{1}$.		
After 1.5 hours, Maxwell was 82.5 miles from home.		
The relationship between time driving and distance travelled is proportional.		
Maxwell travels at a constant speed of 55 mph.		
The y-intercept for this relationship is (0, 55)		

Answers:
False
True
True
True
False

8. The Holden Corporation sells items that are shaped like cubes. Select Yes or No if the volumes below represent cubes with integer side lengths.　　(8.EE.2)

Volumes	Yes	No
27 in.³		
6.25 m³		
1000 cm.³		
33 in.³		
4.8 yd³		
8 in.³		

Answers:
Yes
No
Yes
No
No
Yes

9. A shipping company has a stack of boxes. The stack measures x boxes wide, x boxes high and x boxes long. Select Yes or No if the equations could represent the total number of boxes.

(8.EE.2)

Equations	Yes	No
$64 = x^3$		
$8000 = x^3$		
$24 = x^3$		
$100 = x^3$		
$125 = x^3$		
$9 = x^3$		

Answers:
Yes
Yes
No
No
Yes
No

10. Select True or False for each inequality below.

(8.EE.4)

Equations	True	False
$4.7 \times 10^4 > 4.7 \times 10^{-4}$		
$3.2 \times 10^{-2} < 3.2 \times 10^{-3}$		
$1.4 \times 10^{-1} > 1.4 \times 10^{-2}$		
$2.5 \times 10^{-5} < 2.5 \times 10^{-1}$		

Answers:
True
False
True
True

11. Select True or False for each equation below.

(8.EE.1)

Equations	True	False
$2^{-3} \times 2^{-2} = 2^{-5} = \dfrac{1}{32}$		
$3^{-7} \times 3^4 = 3^{-2} = \dfrac{1}{9}$		
$5^2 \times 5^{-4} = 5^{-2} = \dfrac{1}{25}$		
$4^{-1} \times 4^{-2} = 4^{-3} = \dfrac{1}{12}$		

Answers:
True
False
True
False

12. Sort the following equations into the category that correctly shows the solution of the equation. (8.EE.7)

Write the **letter** of the equation in the box.

Equation A	Equation B	Equation C	Equation D	Equation E
$5x + 2.5 = 10$	$2(x - 2) = -2x - 10$	$-3 = -8x + 9$	$-x + 4.5 = -4x$	$6x + 4 = 4x + 7$

Solution $x = -1.5$	Solution $x = \dfrac{3}{2}$

Answers
Solution $x = -1.5$
 Cards B and D
Solution $x = \dfrac{3}{2}$
 Cards A, C and E

13. Sort each expression into the correct category. (8.EE.1)

Write the letter of the expression in the box.

Expression A	Expression B	Expression C
$\dfrac{4^9}{4^{10}}$	$\dfrac{4^{10}}{4^9}$	$4^6(4^{-4})$

Expression D	Expression E	Expression F
$(4^2 \cdot 4)^0$	$(-4)^3$	$\dfrac{4^{-2}}{4^{-4}}$

Answers
 Less than 4
Cards A, D E
Equal to 4
Card B
Greater than 4
Cards F and C

Less than 4	Equal to 4	Greater than 4

14. Circle all the equations that are parallel to the line: $y = 1.5x + 2$.   (8.EE.6)

$$4 = -1.5x - y \qquad y = \frac{6}{4}x + 2.1 \qquad y = \frac{3}{2}x \qquad y - 1.5x = 5$$

Answers
Circle last three equations.

15. Otto buys two picture frames. Each picture frame is shaped like an equilateral polygon as shown in the picture below. The two picture frames have the same perimeter. Select whether each statement is True or False.   (8.EE.7)

Answers
False
True
True
True

Statement	True	False
The value of x is 12.		
The side length of the rhombus is 9.		
The equation $3(x+5) - 4(x+2) = 0$ can be used to solve for x.		
The perimeter of the triangular picture frame is 36.		

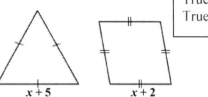

$x + 5$ $x + 2$

16. Ramone and Felix are both electricians. Ramone charges a flat fee of $63 plus $36 per hour. Felix charges $50 per hour. Select whether each statement below is True or False.   (8.EE.7)

Statement	True	False
For 3 hours of work Ramone charges $108.		
For 7 hours of work, Felix charges $350.		
Both electricians charge the same amount for 4 hours of work.		
The equation $50x = 63 + 36x$ can be used to find the number of hours, x, for which the total cost is the same for both electricians.		
Ramone's total cost is less than Felix's total cost for a job that takes 3 hours to complete.		

Answers
False
True
False
True
False.

17. The perimeter of a rectangular garden is 56 feet. The length of the garden is $(3x + 1)$ feet and the width of the garden is $(2x - 3)$ feet.　　　　　　　　(8.EE.7)
Select if each statement below is True or False.

Statement	True	False
The width of the garden is 9 feet.		
The equation $(3x + 1) + (2x - 3) = 56$ can be solved to find the value of x.		
The length of the garden is 19 feet.		
The equation $56 - 2(3x + 1) = 2(2x - 3)$ can be solved to find the value of x.		
The garden is a square.		

Answers
True
False
True
True
False

18. Select if each equation has No Solution, One Solution or Infinite Solutions.　　　(8.EE. 7)

Equation	No Solution	One Solution	Infinite Solutions
$7 - 2x - 3 = 2(2 - x)$			
$4x - (-2x + 4) = 10x + 4$			
$-6x - 3x + x - 2 = 2(-4x - 1)$			
$5 - 4(2x - 3) = -8x + 7$			
$-5(2x - 3) = 4x - 9$			

Answers:
Infinite Solutions
One Solution
Infinite Solutions
No Solution
One Solution

19. Sort the following pairs of equations into the category that correctly describes if the lines are parallel or perpendicular.

(8.EE.8)

Write the **letter** of the equations in the box.

Equations A	Equations B	Equations C	Equations D	Equations E
$y = 2x - 3$ $y = -\dfrac{1}{2}x + 2$	$y = -0.5x + 8$ $y - 4 = 2x$	$y = -3x - 2$ $y = -3x + 5$	$y = 2.5x - 1$ $y = -0.4x$	$y = \dfrac{8}{2}x + 12$ $y = 4x - 4$

Parallel Lines	Perpendicular Lines

Answers
Parallel Lines
   Cards C and E
Perpendicular Lines
Cards A, B and D

20. Select Yes or No if the point (2,3) is a solution for each system of equations in the table below.

(8.EE. 8)

Equations	Yes (2,3) is a Solution	No (2,3) is not a Solution
$y = x + 1$ $y = 0.5x + 2$		
$y - x = 1$ $2x - 1 = y$		
$y + x = 5$ $2y - 2x = 1$		
$y = 3x - 3$ $y = 5x - 7$		
$y = 2x - 1$ $y = 3x$		

Answers:
Yes
Yes
No
Yes
No

21. Select Equal or Not Equal if each equations in the table below is equal to the equation:
$k = 3m - 6$.

(8.EE. 7)

Equations	Equal to $k = 3m - 6$	Not Equal to $k = 3m - 6$
$\dfrac{1}{3}k + 2 = m$		
$\dfrac{k+6}{3} = m$		
$m = \dfrac{6-k}{3}$		
$k + 6 = m$		
$\dfrac{k}{3} + 2 = m$		

Answers:
Equal
Equal
Not Equal
Not Equal
Equal

22. Circle all the slopes that are equal to the slope between the two points:

(8.EE.6)

(2, -2) and (8, 1)

$\dfrac{4}{2}$ $\dfrac{3}{6}$ $\dfrac{1}{2}$ 0.5 $\dfrac{-5}{-10}$ 2

Answers:
Circle
$\dfrac{3}{6}$ $\dfrac{1}{2}$ 0.5 $\dfrac{-5}{-10}$

23. Select Yes or No if each point lies on the graph of: $6x - 4 = y$.

Point	Yes on the graph	Not on the graph
(2, 10)		
(1, 2)		
(0, -4)		
(-5, -26)		
(-2, -16)		

Answers:
No
Yes
Yes
No
Yes

24. Select Yes or No if each equation in the table can be used to represent this problem:
In 10 years, Rasha will be 49 years old.   Let a = Rasha's age now.

(8.EE.7)

Equation	Yes	Not
$49 + a = 10$		
$10 + a = 49$		
$a = 49 - 10$		
$10 - a = 49$		
$49 - a = 10$		

Answers:
No
Yes
Yes
No
Yes

25. A system of equations has No Solution. Select if each statement below is True or False.

(8.EE.8)

Statement	True	False
Both equations have the same slopes but different y-intercepts.		
The lines are parallel.		
Both equations have the different slopes and different y-intercepts.		
The lines intersect at one point.		
Both lines pass through the origin.		

Answers
True
True
False
False
False

26. Select Yes or No if each point is a solution to: $\frac{x}{4} - 3 = y$.

(8.EE.6)

Point	Yes is a solution	No is not a solution
(4, -2)		
(-8, -5)		
(1, 1)		
(20, 2)		
(12, 0)		

Answers:
Yes
Yes
No
Yes
Yes

27. Select True or False for each statement below.

(8.EE.6)

Statement	True	False
The slope of a line with the points (1, 2) and (4, 3) on it is positive.		
The y-intercept in $y=3x-1$ is the point (0, 1)		
The unit rate of $y = \frac{2}{3}x$ is $\frac{2}{3}$.		
The line y= -3 has a negative slope.		
The equation $x - y = 5$ has a positive slope.		
The y-intercept of $x - y = 5$ is the point (0, -5)		

Answers:
True
False
True
False
True
True

28. Sort the following cards into the correct category. Write the letter of the card in the category.

(8.EE.6)

Card A	Card B	Card C	Card D	Card E	Card F
$y = \dfrac{7}{4}x - 2$	$y = -\dfrac{5}{6}x$	$\dfrac{-7}{8}x = y$	$y = -7$	$y = 3x + 4$	$4 = y - x$

Positive Slope	Negative Slope	Zero Slope

Answers:
Positive Slope
Cards A E F
Negative Slope
Cards B C
Zero Slope
Card D

29. Select Yes or No if each problem below has a slope equal to the slope in the equation:

$$y = \frac{3}{6}x + 4$$

(8.EE.6)

Yes	No	Problem
		$y = \dfrac{-1}{2}x - 5$
		Points (7, 2) and (-1, -2)
		$y = 0.5x + 2.$
		$\dfrac{-5}{10}x + y = 6$
		$y = 3 - 2x$

Answers:
No
Yes
Yes
Yes
No

30. Select True or False for each statement.

(8.EE.6)

Statement	True	False
The slope of $y = \frac{3}{4}x + 2$ is steeper than of $y = -\frac{3}{4}x + 2$.		
The y-intercepts are the same in the equations: $y = \frac{4}{5}x + 3$ and $y = 0.8x - 3$.		
A line with a slope of zero is a horizontal line.		
$x + y = 8$ is the same equation as $y = 8 - x$.		
The slope of $y = -\frac{7}{8}x + 1$ is steeper than the slope of $y = -\frac{2}{3}x + 2$.		

Answers:
False
False
True
True
True

Functions

1. The cost at Playland to use the Internet includes a flat fee plus a constant rate per minute, as shown in the table below. (8.F.4)

Time (minutes), x	1	5	10	15
Total Cost ($), y	$1.70	$2.50	$3.50	$4.50

Answers:
False
True
True
False

Select if each statement is True or False.

Statement	True	False
8 minutes of Internet use costs $3.00.		
The constant rate of change is $0.20 per minute.		
The flat fee is $1.50.		
Each minute of Internet use costs $1.50.		

2. The table shows the cost of buying different amounts of ham at the deli. The total cost is a direct variation of the number of pounds purchased. (8.F.4)

Weight (lbs.), x	2	4	10
Cost, $, y	13	26	65

Answers:
CoP = $6.50 per pound
$y=6.5x$

What is the constant of proportionality? _____

Write an equation in $y = mx$ form to represent this situation. _____

3. Use the graph to determine if each statement below is True or False.   (8.F.4)

Statement	True	False
The slope of the line is $\frac{75}{2}$.		
In 4 hours, the Townsend family travelled 150 miles.		
It took the Townsend family about 1.5 hours to travel 27 miles.		
The y-intercept is (0, 0).		

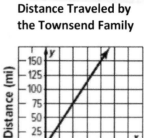

Distance Traveled by the Townsend Family

Answers:
True
True
False
True

4. An appliance store is having a 20% sale on all items in the store. Mr. Grande has a coupon for $15 off. The function $f(x) = 0.8x - 15$ represents the final cost after the discount and coupon are applied for an item priced x dollars. Complete the function table below.   (8.F.1, 8.F.4)

Input	Output
$150	
	$65
$372	
	$437

Answers:
$105
$100
$282.60
$565

5. Circle each table below if it is a function.

(8.F.1)

Table One		Table Two		Table Three		Table Four		Table Five	
x	y	x	y	x	y	x	y	x	y
-8	0	-2	4	-1	4	0	2	-2	2
-3	5	-2	3	0	8	1	4	-1	1
2	10	0	2	1	12	2	6	0	0
4	10	2	1	2	16	2	7	1	1

Answers:
Functions are:
Table One
Table Three
Table Five

6. Select Yes or No if the following points are correct values for the function: $y = \frac{1}{4}x$.

(8.F.1)

Points	Yes	No
(4, 1)		
(-4, -4)		
(0, 0)		
(3, 12)		
(-2, -0.5)		

Answers:
Yes
No
Yes
No
Yes

7. Select if the slope of the equation given is greater or not greater than the slope of the line in the graph.

(8.F.1)

Equation	Slope is Greater	Slope is Not Greater
$y = x + 6$		
$y = -3x$		
$y = 0.8x + 3$		
$y = \frac{1}{2}x - 2$		
$y = 2.6x + 1$		

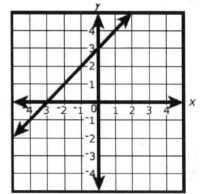

Answers:
Not greater
Greater
Not greater
Not greater
Greater

Geometry

1. $\overline{CD}$ and $\overline{AB}$ are plotted on the coordinate plane below. Select whether each statement is True or False. (8.G.1)

Statement	True	False
The image of point C reflected over the y-axis is (-1, -2).		
The slope of $\overline{AB}$ = the slope of $\overline{CD}$ but the direction is different.		
$\overline{AB} \perp \overline{CD}$		
$\overline{CD}$ can be mapped onto $\overline{AB}$ by a reflection over the y-axis then a reflection over the x-axis.		
The slope of $\overline{AB}$ is positive and the slope of $\overline{CD}$ is negative.		

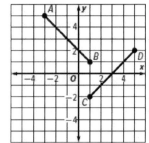

Answers:
True
False
True
False
False

2. A triangular flag *GHF* is mapped on the coordinate plane below. The flag is reflected across the y-axis and is then translated 4 units down and 3 units right to form _____. (8.G.2)
Select whether each statement is True or False.

Statement	True	False
The image of point G is G' (-4,1).		
The image of point H is H' (2, -3).		
The image of point F is F' (0,-1).		
The slopes of $\overline{FH}$ and $\overline{F'H'}$ are reciprocals.		
Triangle *GHF* is congruent to triangle *G'H'F'*		

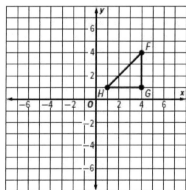

Answers:
False
True
False
True
True

3. Beef stew is available in two different-sized cans. Nick's Beef Stew is a 90-ounce can and is sold for $12.50 per can. The can has a diameter of 6 inches and a height of 4.2 inches. Ray's Beef Stew is a 55-ounce can and is sold for $6.02 per can. This can has a diameter of 4.2 inches and a height of 6 inches. Select whether each statement is True or False.   (8.G.9)

Statement	True	False
The volume of Nick's Beef Stew is about 118.69 cubic inches.		
Ray's Beef Stew is the better buy because it is about 11 cents per ounce.		
The volume of Ray's Beef Stew is about 3 times the volume of Nick's Beef Stew.		
The difference in the price per ounce of the two cans is about 3 cents.		

Answers:
True
True
False
True

4. A square is mapped on a coordinate plane. Mary uses square *SPRQ* and the rule (-0.5*x*, -0.5*y*) to draw another square.   (8.G.3)

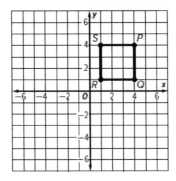

Select whether each statement is True or False.

Statement	True	False
The square $S'P'R'Q'$ is smaller in size than square *SPRQ*.		
The image of point P is P' (-2, -2).		
The image of point R is R' (0.5, 0.5)		
Square *SPRQ* and its image are congruent polygons.		
The length of *SP* is twice the length of $S'P'$.		

Answers:
True
True
False
False
True

5. Triangle ABC and Triangle DEF are plotted on a coordinate plane.   (8.G.1)

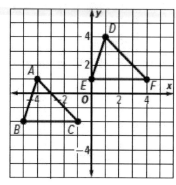

Select whether each statement is True or False.

Statement	True	False
The area of Triangle *DEF* is 12 square units.		
The height of triangle *ABC* is 3.		
Triangle *ABC* can be mapped onto Triangle *DEF* by the translation $(x + 3, y + 5)$		
The length of *BC* = the length of *EF*.		
Triangle *DEF* can be mapped onto Triangle *ABC* by the translation $(x - 5, y - 3)$		

Answers:
False
True
False
True
True

6. Use the description of each triangle to determine if it is a right triangle or not.

(8.G.7)

Statement	Yes forms a right triangle	No does not form a right triangle
Triangle with side lengths 6, 6 and $6\sqrt{2}$.		
Perimeter of 12, two sides are 4 and 5.		
Triangle with sides 5, 8 and 13.		
Perimeter of 36, two sides are 9 and 12.		
Triangle with sides 10, 5 and $5\sqrt{5}$		

Answers:
Yes
Yes
No
Yes
Yes

The Number System

1. Select whether the number described in each statement is rational or irrational.

(8.NS.1)

Statement	Rational	Irrational
Jack calculates each side length of a square as $3\sqrt{16}$ meters.		
The length of a rope measures $42.\overline{6}$ cm.		
The circumference of a circular frame is 5π inches.		
The depth of a canyon is -85.75 feet.		

Answers:
Rational
Rational
Irrational
Rational

2. Mrs. Foster gave her math students a task work 100 points. (8.NS.1)

These are 4 of the student scores:

☐ Sylvester earned a score of 88.6%,

☐ Dana earned a score of $\dfrac{89}{100}$ points,

☐ Irma earned a score of $\sqrt{7569}$ points

☐ Paul earned a score of that was 1.4 percent less than Sylvester's percent.

Answers:
Check student accuracy. Sylvester should be located at 88.6, Dana at 89, Irma at 87 and Paul at 87.2

Plot these points on the number line below. Use the first letter of the student's name to label the points.

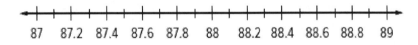

87   87.2 87.4 87.6 87.8   88   88.2 88.4 88.6 88.8   89

3. The number line below shows four points labeled *A*, *B*, *C* and *D*. Select whether each statement is True or False. (8.NS.2)

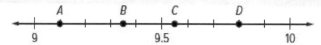

Statement	True	False
The value of $\sqrt{86.49}$ is between points *A* and *B*.		
The coordinate of point C is greater than $\sqrt{95}$.		
The coordinate of Point D is less than $\sqrt{99}$.		

Answers:
True
False
True

4. Select whether each statement is True or False. (8.NS.2)

Statement	True	False
$\sqrt{5+16}$ is irrational.		
0.5274 is rational.		
$0.\overline{36}$ is irrational.		
0.234234234…is irrational.		
$\sqrt{2}$ is irrational.		

Answers:
True
True
False
False
True

5. The number line shows four points labeled *A*, *B*, *C* and *D*. Select whether each statement is True or False. (8.NS.2)

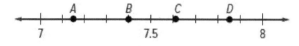

Answers:
False
True
True

Statement	True	False
The value of $\sqrt{63}$ is between points *C* and *D*.		
The coordinate of point B is greater than $\sqrt{50}$.		
The coordinate of Point A is less than $\sqrt{55}$.		

Grade Level **8**

NUMERACY
RESOURCE

Problem Solving ANSWERS

The Number System

1. Tanya and Vinny are having a contest to see who can rake the greater area of lawn over one week. The table shows the area in acres they raked each day.   (8.NS.1)

Day	Tanya	Vinny
Sunday	$1\frac{1}{4}$ acres	$\frac{6}{5}$ acres
Monday	0.6 acres	$\frac{1}{2}$ acre
Tuesday	30% of an acre	0.34 of an acre
Wednesday	20% of an acre	$\frac{1}{3}$ acre
Thursday	$\frac{13}{25}$ of an acre	0.58 acres
Friday	75% of an acre	$\frac{2}{3}$ of an acre
Saturday	1 acre	1.1 acres

Answers:
Part A:
Tanya – Sunday, Monday, Friday
Vinny – Tuesday, Wednesday, Thursday, Saturday
Part B: Vinny
Tanya raked about 4.62 acres. Vinny about 4.72.
Part C:
Vinny's total is a 0.1 acre difference.

Part A: Sort each day into one of the two categories according to who raked more that day. Write the day of the week in the correct category.

Tanya raked more acres	Vinny raked more acres

Part B: Who won the contest? _____
Part C: How much more did the winner rake? _____

2. Graph the numbers at their approximate locations on the number line.   (8.NS.2)
   Label the location using the point letter.

Point A = $\sqrt{66}$ Point B= -$\sqrt{15}$ Point C= $\sqrt{35}$ Point D= -$\sqrt{10}$

Sample answer:
Point A= 8.1 or just to the right of 8
Point B= -3.8 or just to the right of -4
Point C= 5.9 or just to the left of 6
Point D= -3.1 or just to the left of -3

Expressions and Equations

1. Kevin's Cab Company charges $6.00 per ride plus $2.50 per mile traveled. Kathy's Cab Company charges $3.00 per ride and $3.00 per mile traveled. (8.EE.7)

> **Part A:** Write an equation to find *m*, the number of miles for which the total cost is the same for both companies.

> **Part B:** Solve your equation to find the number of miles.

> Sample Answers:
> Part A: One equation would be:
> $6 + 2.5m = 3 + 3m$
> Note – could be a system.
> Part B: 6 miles

2. David purchased a storage cube that has a volume of 12 cubic feet. He wants to put the cube on a shelf that is 25 inches below the ceiling.

(8.EE.2)

> Will the cube fit? _____
> Explain your reasoning.

> Sample answer:
> $V = l^3$ so cube root of 12 equals 2.3 feet
> Each side of the cube is about 2.3 feet x 12 = 27.6 inches. No the cube will not fit on the shelf.

3. Polly ran 3 times as many miles as Michael. Michael ran 10 fewer miles than Polly. The number of miles run by each person can be modeled by the system of equations shown below, where *y* represents Polly's miles and *x* represents the number of miles Michael ran.

(8.EE.8)

$$y = 3x \qquad y = x + 10$$

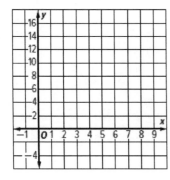

> **Part A:** Graph the equations on the coordinate plane. Label the intersection.

> Sample Answers:
> Part A: Check graph for accuracy
> Part B: (5, 15)

> **Part B:** What is the solution to the system? _____

4. Tracy and her younger sister, Heather, are running a 120-meter race. Tracy runs at a steady rate of 3.5 meters per second. Heather runs at a steady rate of 2 meters per second.

(8.EE.5, 8.EE.7)

Part A: How long will it take each person to finish the race?

Part B: Tracy wants to win the race but only by 5 seconds. She is going to give her sister a 30 meter, 40 meter or 50 meter head start.

Which head start allows Tracy to win the race within 5 seconds of her sister's time?

Sample Answers:
 Part A: Tracy will finish in 34.3 seconds. Students may write 35 sec. here. Heather needs 60 sec.
Part B: Heather needs the 40 m head start if students use 35 sec for Tracy, if they keep the 34.3 then she needs the 50 m start to finish in 35 sec.

5. The area of each small square in the figures below is 49 square units.   (8.EE.2)

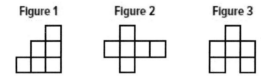

Part A: What do you notice about the areas of the 3 figures? _____

_____

Part B: What is the perimeter of each figure? Show your work here:

Sample answer:
 Part A: All the areas are equal since each figure has 6 squares.
Part B: Figure 1: 12x 7 = 84 units
Figures 2 & 3: 14 x 7 = 98 units.

6. Franklin works as a sales person. He earns $600 per week plus an 8% commission on his total sales. (8.EE.7)

Part A: Last week he had a total sales of $4,000. What was his total earnings?

Part B: This week he wants his sales to increase from last week to this week by an additional $800. How much more will his total earnings be this week compared to last week?

> Sample answer:
> Part A: 4000x 0.08=$320 + 600= $920
> Part B:
> 4800x0.08=$384+600=$984
> $984-920=$64 more

7. Julia has a storage cube with a volume of 27 cubic feet. She has a shelf that is 35 inches from the ceiling. (8.EE.2)

Will the cube fit? _____

Explain how you know.

> Sample answer:
> No the cube will not fit. The cube root of 27 is 3 feet which is each dimension. 3 feet is 36 inches so the cube is too big.

8. What is the measure of the largest angle in this triangle?

(8.EE.7)

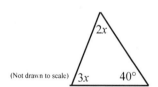

(Not drawn to scale)

Show your work here.

> Sample answer:
> 180-40=140
> 5x=140 so   x=28°
> 3x=84° the largest angle

9. The chess team has 35 female members. The ratio of females to males on the team is 7 to 5. How many members are on the chess team in all? (8.EE.7)

Show your work here.

Sample answer:
$$\frac{35}{x} = \frac{7}{5}$$ 7x=175 x=25 males
Total members = 35 + 25 = 60 members

10. A park in Canada is in the shape of a rectangle. The length is 2.4×10^5 feet and the width is 3.1×10^3 feet. One acre measures 4.356×10^4 square feet. (8.EE.4)

About how many acres does the park cover? Round your answer to the nearest hundredth.

Show your work here.

Sample answer:
$(2.4 \times 3.1 \times 10^5 \times 10^3) = 744 \times 10^6 \div 4.356 \times 10^4 =$ 17,079.89 acres

11. At one sports club, $\frac{5}{6}$ of the people were playing volleyball. After 2 more people joined the people playing volleyball, there was a total of 27 people playing volleyball. How many people in all were at the sports club? (8.EE.7)

Part A: Circle all the equations that can be used to solve this problem.

$$\frac{5}{6}x - 2 = 27 \qquad \frac{5}{6}x = 25 \qquad \frac{5}{6}(x+2) = 27$$

$$27 - 2 = \frac{5}{6}x \qquad \frac{5}{6}x + 2x = 27 \qquad 27 = \frac{5}{6}x + 2$$

Part B: How many people in all were at the sports club?

Sample answer:
Circle: $\frac{5}{6}x = 25$ $27 - 2 = \frac{5}{6}x$ $27 = \frac{5}{6}x + 2$

Solution: There's 30 people.

12. The table shows expressions to represent the number of middle school students enrolled in different clubs. The number of students enrolled in the Drama and Tech Clubs equals the students in the Adventure and Math Clubs. (8.EE.7)

Club	Number of Students
Drama Club	$2n - 14$
Tech Club	$2(3n - 15)$
Adventure Club	$\frac{2}{3}n + 2$
Math Club	$5n - 4$

Sample answer:

$$2n - 14 + 2(3n - 15) = \frac{2}{3}n + 2 + 5n - 4$$

$$2\frac{1}{3}n = 42 \qquad n = 18$$

Drama Cub= 22   Tech Club= 78
Adventure Club=14   Math Club= 86
Total of 200 students.

How many students are in each Club? How many student in all are in the 4 Clubs?

Show your work here.

13. The table below shows the total distance Mrs. Brockton drove last week. (8.EE.7)

Day	Sunday	Monday	Tuesday	Wednesday	Thursday	Friday	Saturday
Miles	10.5	9.75	9.5	10.25	10.75	12	9.25

The total distance Mrs. Brockton drove last week is $\frac{3}{4}$ of the total distance she drove this week.

Part A: Write an equation that can be used to find the total distance, d, Mrs. Brockton drove this week.

Part B: Solve your equation to find the total miles driven this week.

Sample answer:
One possible equation:

Part A: $(10.5+9.75+9.5+10.25+10.75+12+9.25) = \frac{3}{4}x$

Part B: $72 = \frac{3}{4}x$ $x = 96$ miles this week

14. Marty's Online Shopping Company uses boxes like the one shown below to ship purchases to their customers. (8.EE.7)

Part A: The shipping box needs 3,528 square centimeters of cardboard to make its six sides, without overlap. What is the height of the box?
Use the formula for the surface area of a prism $SA = 2wh + 2lw + 2lh$ to write an equation, then find the box height.

24 cm
36 cm

Part B: Would packing material with a volume of 13,000 cubic centimeters fit inside this box? Explain why or why not.

Sample answer:
One possible equation:
Part A: $3528 = 2(24)h + 2(36)(24) + 2(36)h$
$3528 = 48h + 1728 + 72h$
$1800 = 120h$ $h = 15cm$
Part B: $V = (15)(24)(36) = 12,960$ No a volume of 13,000 will not fit.

15. At Hastings School, $\frac{1}{6}$ of the girls had retakes of their school photo. Twenty girls had retakes done. Eight boys had retakes, which was $\frac{2}{15}$ of the boys at the school. How many students are at Hastings School?

(8.EE.7)

Show your work here.

Sample answer:
$\frac{1}{6}x = 20$ so there's 120 girls.
$\frac{2}{15}x = 8$ so there's 60 boys. Total 180.

16. The height of a tree after x years is $1.8x + 3$. How many years will it take for the tree to be 30 feet tall?   (8.EE.7)

Show your work here.

Sample answer:
   $1.8x + 3 = 30$ $x = 15$ years

17. A boat traveled x miles per hour upstream for 4 hours. On the return trip, it traveled 2.5 mph faster. The return trip took 3 hours. What was the round trip distance the boat traveled?

(8.EE.7)

Show your work here.

Sample answer:
  $4x = 3(x+2.5)$
  $4x = 3x + 7.5$ $x = 7.5$ mph
  $D = (4 \times 7.5) \times 2 = 60$ miles

18. Shari wrote the number of hours she ran each day this week in the chart.

(8.EE.7)

Day	Miles
Monday	1.5
Tuesday	0.75
Wednesday	1.25
Thursday	2.5
Friday	x

Sample answer:
$(6 + x) \div 5 = 1.6$
$X = 2$ miles

How many miles does she need to run to average 1.6 miles over the five days?

Show your work here.

19. The table shows Jolene's first six quiz scores in science. After Quiz 1 she stayed each week for extra help with the teacher. What is the rate of change from week 2 to week 6?

(8.EE.7)

Weekly Quiz Number	Score out of 100 points
1	70
2	68
3	72
4	75
5	81
6	93

Sample answer:
Week 6 = 93
 Week 2 = 68
Difference
24 ÷4= 6 points per week

Functions

1. Joan kicked a ball. The path of the ball can be modeled by the equation:
$y= 1.5x^2$. (8.F.3)

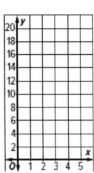

Part A: Make a table of values of x from 0 to 3.

Part B: Graph the path of the kicked ball.

Part C: Is the graph linear? _____

Justify your answer with at least 2 reasons.

Part A:
(0, 0) (1, 1.5) (2,6) (3, 13.5)
Part B: check graph for accuracy
Part C: Not linear
The graph curves and there is no constant change between data points.

2. The height of a dime dropped from a 144-foot tall building roof is modeled by the function $h = -16t^2 + 144$, where t is the time in seconds and h is the height of the dime as it falls to the ground. (8.F.1, 8.F.3)

Part A: Complete the table of values for the dime as it falls.

Time, t	0	0.5	1	1.5	2	2.5	3
Height, h							

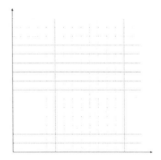

Part B: Graph the function on the coordinate plane to the right.

Part C: How long does it take for the dime to reach the ground?

Sample Answers:
 Part A: Heights are:
144, 140, 128, 108, 80, 44, 0
Part B: Check graph for accuracy.
Part C: 3 seconds.

3. Mr. Stevens is filling his child's pool. The pool has a capacity of 240 gallons. Every minute, a constant 4.5 gallons of water flows into the pool.

(8.F.4)

Part A: Complete the table to show the number of gallons or minutes.

Minutes	Gallons
1	
2	
5	
	36
	45

Sample Answers:
 Part A:
1 min   4.5 gal
2 min   9 gal
5 min   22.5 gal
8 min   36 gal
10 min   45 gal
Part B: 54 gal
Part C: 54 + 126 =
180 ÷240 = 75% full

Part B: How many gallons of water will be added after 12 minutes? _____

Part C: The pool started with 126 gallons of water. After 12 minutes of filling the pool, what percent of the full capacity does the water in the pool represent?

4. Kate and Ruth ran a race. Ruth gets a 44 foot head start. The distance, y (in feet) Ruth runs after x seconds is represented by the linear function: $y = 16x + 44$. The table shows the distances Kate runs.

(8.F.2)

Time, sec. x	2	4	10
Distance, feet y	36	72	190

Sample Answers:
Part A: Kate runs 18 feet per second – faster than 14.
Part B
16x+44= 18x   x=22 sec
Part C: 18 x 22 = 396 feet

Part A: Who runs faster?

 Explain how you know.

Part B: After how many seconds will they be at the same distance?

 Show your work here.

Part C: At what distance will they be in the same place?

 Show your work here.

Geometry and Statistics

1. The picture below shows how a pole broke during a winter storm. (8.G.7)

How tall was the original pole?

Show your work.

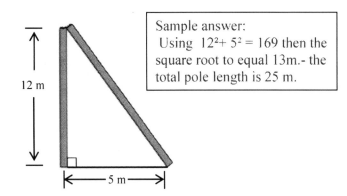

12 m

5 m

Sample answer:
Using $12^2 + 5^2 = 169$ then the square root to equal 13m.- the total pole length is 25 m.

2. Donna dilates the rectangle below using a scale factor of 25%. (8.G.4)

12 cm

20 cm

What is the area of the dilated rectangle?

Sample answer:
25% is ¼ .
¼ x 12 = 3   ¼ x 20 = 5
A=3x5 = 15 sq cm

3. A rectangular sports arena measures 100 yards by 50 yards. Debbie ran from one corner to the opposite corner along the diagonal of the rectangle. Arthur ran along the length and then the width to the opposite corner. (8.G.7)

Part A: Who ran further?

Part B: By how many more yards?
Round your answer to the nearest tenth of a yard.

Sample Answers:
Part A: Debbie: $50^2 + 100^2 = 12,500$
$\sqrt{12500} = 111.8$ yards
Arthur: 150 yards ran further
Part B: 150-111.8 = 38.2 more yards

4. Benita surveys some friends to see the number of hours they studied for the History test. The results are recorded in the table. (8.SP.1)

Time (h)	4	0	2.5	1	3	1.5
Test Score	95	65	75	85	90	80

Part A: Construct a scatterplot of the data.

Part B: Describe one pattern you see in the data.

_____

_____

_____

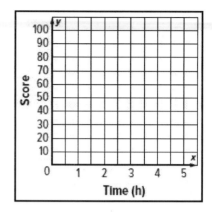

Possible answer:
 Part A: check accuracy of graphed points
 Part B: There is a positive correlation.

5. Maple Avenue and Pine Street are parallel. Ridge Road is a straight road that crosses each of them. The town planner needs to find the measures of the angles at each intersection. (8.G.5)

Find the measures of the labeled angles.

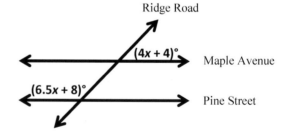

Sample answer:
 $6.5x+8 + 4x + 4 = 180$
 $10.5x = 168$
 $X = 16$
 $4x+4 = 68°$ $6.5x+8 = 112°$

6. An apartment building measures 36 feet by 29 feet as shown in the picture below.

(8.G.7)

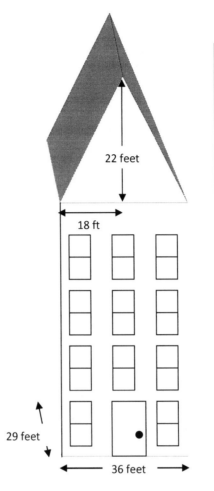

22 feet

18 ft

29 feet

36 feet

Sample answer:

$$22^2 + 18^2 = x^2$$

$$484 + 324 = x^2$$

$$808 = x^2$$

$$x = 28.4\,ft$$

The area of one side of the roof is 28.4 x 29 = 824.5 ft². so
the total area of the roof is 824.5 x 2 = 1648.9 ft².

Since the shingles are 15 ft by 15 ft.. each shingle covers
225 square feet of the roof.
The number of packages of shingles the owner will need is
1648.9 ÷ 225 = 7.3 ≈ 8 packages of shingles.

Total cost of shingles is 8 packages x $50 = $400.

The owner needs to cover the roof, the shaded section in the picture, with shingles. A package of shingles costs $50 and will cover a 15-foot by 15-foot area.

How much will it cost for enough packages of shingles to cover the roof? _____

Show your work here.

7. A triangle has two sides whose measures are 15 feet and 25 feet. The perimeter of the triangle is 60 feet.

(8.G.7)

Is the triangle a right triangle?

Show your work here.

Sample answer:
Part A: 60 -25 -15 = missing side
    Side is 20
$20^2 + 15^2 = x^2$
$400 + 225 = x^2$
$625 = x^2$
$x = 25 ft$
Yes it is a right triangle.

8. The area of the square pictured below is 1,296 in².

(8.G.7)

4x

What is the length of the side of the square?

Sample answer:
16x² = 1296
x² = 81 so x equals 9.
The side is 36 in.

9. Two planes are flying in the same direction towards the same tower at the same airport. Plane A's altitude is 6.4 km. high. Plane B is 2 km further away from the airport tower and its altitude is 2.8 km.

(8.G.7)

Which plane is further in distance from the base of the airport tower?

Plane A
6.4 km

Plane B
2.8 km

Airport Tower   4 km   2 km

Sample answer:
4² + 6.4² =56.96
Square root of 56.96 is about 7.5 km
6²+2.8²= 43.84
 Square root of 43.84 is about 6.6 km

Grade Level **8**

NUMERACY
RESOURCE

Reasoning
ANSWERS

1. Rodney had to compare the following numbers. (8.EE.1)

$$\text{Number A} = 5 \times 10^{-2} \qquad \text{Number B} = 3 \times 10^{-4}$$

Rodney says Number B is greater because the negative exponents just mean the numbers have a negative value. The exponent 10^4 is larger in Number B than the exponent 10^2 in Number A so

$$5 \times 10^{-2} < 3 \times 10^{-4}.$$

Explain what math mistake Rodney made and write the correct comparison.

> One possible Answer:
> Rodney's mistake is that he did not evaluate the negative exponents correctly.
> $5 \times 10^{-2} = 5 \times .01 = 0.05$
>
> $3 \times 10^{-4} = 3 \times 0.0001 = 0.0003$

2. Molly had to find $\sqrt{1681}$. Her work is shown below.

> One possible Answer:
> Square roots cannot be written in equivalent expanded form. Correct answer is 41.
> Checking $49 \times 49 = 2401$ not correct.
> Check with another example
> $\sqrt{400} = 20$ not $\sqrt{4} + \sqrt{100} = 12$

Step 1 $\qquad \sqrt{1681} = \sqrt{1600} + \sqrt{81}$

Step 2 $\qquad\qquad\quad = 40 + 9$

Step 3 $\qquad \sqrt{1681} = 49$

Explain the math mistake Molly made. Provide the correct solution.

3. A square table has an area of 39 square feet. Joey says the side length has to be between 7.5 and 8 feet. Explain if Joey's thinking is correct or not. (8.NS.2)

> One possible Answer:
> The two closest perfect squares are 36 and 49 so it is between 6 and 7 feet. It is closer to 6 than 7 feet.

4. Justin says that you can use the Commutative property for multiplication with square roots. His example is shown below: (8.NS.2)

$3\sqrt{2}$ has the same value as $2\sqrt{3}$.

> One possible Answer:
> The commutative property does not work with square roots.
> $3\sqrt{2} = 3 \times 1.414 = 4.242$
> $2\sqrt{3} = 2 \times 1.73 = 3.46$

Explain if Justin's thinking is correct or not.

5. George had to simplify the following problem. His work is shown below.

(8.EE.1)

$$\frac{3^{-2}}{3^{-4}} =$$

Step one: $\frac{1}{3^2} \times \frac{3^4}{1}$

Step two: $\frac{1}{6} \times \frac{12}{1}$

Step three: $\frac{12}{6}$

Step four: 2

> One possible Answer:
> Part A: Step two
> Part B: He computed the exponents incorrectly.
> Part C: Subtract the exponents when dividing
> $3^{-2-(-4)} = 3^2 = 9$
> Or step two:
> $\frac{1}{9} x \frac{81}{1} = 9$

Part A: Which step did George make his <u>first</u> mistake? _____

Part B: What math mistake did George make? _____

_____

Part C: Provide the correct solution and work.

6. Mario's solution to the equation $3y + 8 = 7y + 11$ is shown below.

(8.EE.7)

$$3y + 8 = 7y + 11$$

Step one: $-3y \qquad -3y$

Step two: $8 = 4y + 11$
$\qquad\qquad -8 \qquad\quad -8$

Step three: $4y = 3$

Step four: $\dfrac{4y}{4} = \dfrac{3}{4}$

Step five: $y = \dfrac{3}{4}$

Sample answer:

Part A: Step two

Part B: He should subtract 11 to isolate the variable.

Part C: $-3 = 4y$ so $y = -\dfrac{3}{4}$

Part A: What step did Mario make his <u>first</u> math mistake? _____

Part B: What math mistake did he make? _____

_____

Part C: Provide the correct solution.

7. Nancy's solution to an equation is shown below.

(8.EE.7)

$$6(x - 3) = 4x - 7$$

Step one: $6x - 3 = 4x - 7$
Step two: $-4x \qquad\quad -4x$

Step three: $2x - 3 = 7$
$\qquad\qquad\quad +3 \ +3$
Step four: $2x \quad = 10$

Step five: $\dfrac{2x}{2} = \dfrac{10}{2}$

Step six: $x = 5$

Sample answer:
Part A: Step one
Part B: When multiplying she needed to multiply 6 times (-3)
Part C: $6x - 18 = 4x - 7$
$\qquad\quad 2x - 18 = -7$
$\qquad\qquad + 18 \ +18$
$\qquad\quad 2x = 11$ so $x = 5.5$

Part A: What step did Nancy make her <u>first</u> math mistake? _____

Part B: What math mistake did she make? _____

_____

Part C: Provide the correct solution.

8. Mr. Kroner has a 25-foot ladder and a 30-foot ladder. He claims if you position the 30-foot ladder 15 feet away from the bottom of a building, it will reach no higher than the 25-foot ladder positioned 10 feet away from the bottom of the building.   (8.G.7)

Is Mr. Kroner correct?

Explain how you know.

> One possible Answer:
> No he is not. The 25-foot ladder would be 22.9 feet above the ground while the 30 foot ladder would be 25.9 feet above the ground.

9. Candace's solution to an equation is shown below.
                                                                                     (8.EE.7)

$$-0.5(20x - 6) - 4 = 17$$

Step one: $-9x - 6 - 4 = 17$
Step two: $-9x - 10 = 17$

Step three: $-9x - 10 = 17$
                           $+10 \quad +10$
Step four: $-9x = 27$

Step five: $\dfrac{-9x}{-9} = \dfrac{27}{-9}$

Step six: $x = -3$

> Sample answer:
> Part A: Step one
> Part B: In step 1 -0.5(20x) = 10 x also she needed to multiply (-6) times (-0.5) to get +3
> Part C: -10x + 3 -4 =17
>   -10x -1 = 17
>   -10x= +18
>   so x = -1.8

Part A: What step did Candace make her <u>first</u> math mistake? _____

Part B: What math mistake did she make? _____

Part C: Provide the correct solution.

10. Alex is making a flag in the shape of a trapezoid. The fabric to make the flag has

an area of 56.25 square inches. The formula for finding the area of a trapezoid is: (8.EE.7)

$$A = \frac{1}{2}h(b_1 + b_2).$$

Alex says if he doubles the longer base, then the area of the flag will also double.

Explain if his thinking is correct.

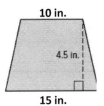

10 in.

4.5 in.

15 in.

| One possible Answer: |
| No he is not correct. The new area would be 90 which is not double 56.25. |

11. Lucy is finding the volume of a cube with an edge length of 4ab. Her work is shown below.
                                                            (8.EE.1)

Step one: V= (4ab)³

Step two: V=(4³)(a³)(b³)

Step three: V= 12 a³b³

| Sample answer: |
| Part A: When multiplying the exponent she did not use 4 as a factor three times. |
| Part B: 64 a³b³ |

Part A: Explain what math mistake Lucy made. _____

Part B: Provide the correct solution.

12. The planet Venus is about 1.1×10^8 km from the sun. The planet Mercury is about 5.8×10^7 km from the sun.

(8.EE.4)

Rona says Mercury is about 5 times farther from the sun than Venus because $5.8 \div 1.1$ is about 5.

Part A: Explain what math mistake Rona made. _____

Part B: Provide the correct solution.

> Sample answer:
> Part A: Venus is farther from the sun when you compare the exponents of 10^8 and 10^7.
> Part B: To compare use equal exponents or use $110 \div 58 = 1.89$ or about 2 times farther from the sun.

13. Harlan says that a triangle with sides that measure 8 cm and 6 cm whose perimeter is 24 cannot be a right triangle because $6^2 + 8^2$ does not equal 24^2.

(8.G.7)

Part A: Explain what math mistake Harlan made. _____

Part B: Provide the correct solution.

> Sample answer:
> Part A: The hypotenuse is not 24 cm.
> Part B
> $24 - 14 = 10$ cm the hypotenuse.
> $6^2 + 8^2 = 10^2$ so it is a right triangle.

14. Devon says that 5 + (*xy*) is equal to (5+ *x*) (5+*y*) because it is an example of the Distributive Property.

(8.EE.7)

Part A: Explain what math mistake Devon made. _____

Part B: Provide the correct solution.

> Sample answer:
> Part A: This is not an example of the Distributive Property.
> Part B
> The solution is 5 + *xy* no simplifying can be done.

15. Vivian and Betsy are writing equations for the line that passes through the points

(-6, 0) and (0. -2).   Their work is shown below.

(8.EE.7)

Vivian's Work

$m= \dfrac{2}{6}$ and *b*= 2

so the equation is

$y= \dfrac{2}{6}x + 2$

Betsy's Work

$m= \dfrac{-2}{6}$ and the *y*-intercept is 0

so the equation is:

$y= \dfrac{-2}{6}x$

Part A: Explain what math error each person made.

Vivian's math error: _____

Betsy's math error: _____

Part B: Provide the correct solution.

> Sample answer:
> Part A:
> Vivian: Both the slope and y-intercept need to be negative
> Betsy: the y-intercept is wrong
> Part B
> Slope $= \dfrac{-2}{6}$ y-intercept = (0, -2)
>
> Equation: $y= \dfrac{-2}{6}x$ -2

CREC Educational Resources

To meet your needs, CREC offers educational resources in both print and digital media, including books, reference guides, manuals, e-books, webinars, and online professional development.

Resources are available on the following topics:

- Children's books
- Early childhood
- Educating struggling learners
- Leadership
- Literacy
- Numeracy
- Paraeducators
- School climate
- School management
- Special education

Excellence in Education

Tom Sullivan
CREC Publishing Services
tosullivan@crec.org
860-240-6625

Made in the USA
Middletown, DE
23 December 2017